The Journey

MARY ANGELINE BELL

INKS & BINDINGS

Inks and Bindings
888-290-5218
www.inksandbindings.com
orders@inksandbindings.com

CONTENTS

DEDICATION

Jasmine, Chloe, Thea
Jesse, Connor
Jessica, Madelyn
Bill, Jennie

MOTHER

My forward steps gave her joy.
My missteps gave her pain.
In a world of strife and suffering
Would I still have hopes that remain?
Now I'm a mother, privileged to love
But vulnerable to grief.
I lift my child in prayer
For a life of hope and belief.

FATHER

He was there for me
When I was unsure of myself,
Believing in my potential,
Helping me go beyond myself to see
A protector, encourager,
And proud to be my dad.
In rough times and in comfort,
Rejoicing when triumphs made me glad.

A JOURNEY

Another trip around the sun.
How was it filled? Was there some fun?
I would not be a recluse, dwelling on the sad.
Life is a journey; let what I've done make me glad.
How many trips this earth will give me, I don't know.
But through each journey, let my wisdom grow.

DAY OF JOY

It was a beautiful day in August. At last, the much-anticipated day had come. My husband and I were to meet our little daughter being brought to us by Holt International Children's Services. She was being flown from Korea to the airport in Eugene, Oregon. The trip from Portland down the I-5 freeway seemed long. When we arrived at the Eugene airport, we knew that our "stork" plane would be a United Airlines flight from San Francisco. We watched two United planes land and passengers disembark. No baby yet. Then a third plane landed. We watched the passengers getting off. The very last were a man carrying a dark-haired baby. We were right at the gate. The moment when the man said, "Here's your little doll," and placed her in my arms will stay in my heart forever.

The man had some papers for us to sign. The fourteen-month-old toddler was officially in our custody. Six months later, a judge would sign some different papers, hand them to us, and exclaim, "She's yours." Of course, we had prepared for months for this day with paperwork and interviews. We had pictures of the child whom we named Janice, and progress reports. But for Janice, it was different. She had been cared for in a foster home, and now she did not understand what was happening to her. She had been whisked away to a strange place with strange people who did not look like the people among whom she had lived. Add to that the fact that she was jet-lagged, and none of us got much sleep that first night. In the morning, we took her out and bought her some shoes. She was just starting to walk,

And she had arrived with only socks on her feet.

A few days later, some friends came to the house with a surprise baby shower.

If a couple is adopting now through Holt, it is required that at least one of the adopting parents go where the child is and spend a few days with the child. Then, when they go to the child's new home, the child knows who he or she is going with. It becomes easier for the child to see the adopting parents as "Mommy" and "Daddy" and no longer strangers.

In the ensuing months, we met other families with children adopted through Holt. The children could learn that there are other families like theirs. These are some of the extras in helping an adopted son or daughter establish his or her identity. Janice, who as a young adult changed her first name to Jennie, is now a grandmother herself. Like each of us, she has had some grief and problems, but I hope that she has seen that life is worth living.

JOURNEY

A babe, a child of my spirit
Growing amid earthly cares and stress,
Dealing with forces that vex and trouble.
Moving toward bonds that might comfort.
Out of the heartache, two children to bless
Moving their way through chaos and rubble.
Finding at last a solace fair,
Sweet comfort of knowing one's own worth,
And sharing joy and kindness on earth.

NUMBERS

How many trips around the sun?
A tax for every trip I've done.
I know not how many remain:
Numbers for pressure sugar and pain.
Numbers for income must fit what I spend.
I can't take with me what's left at the end.
I'll soar with the stars whose numbers are vast,
Till I'm free from earth's numbers: free at last.

$$4 \quad 8 \qquad 100$$
$$+ \quad -$$
$$1000$$
$$\% \quad \$$$
$$E=m(csqared)$$

COMPUTER JOURNEY

Imagine a device that could do calculations in split seconds, at one time within many people's memories; that was an impressive thought. Furthermore, the two-way wrist radio in the Dick Tracy comic strip was the stuff of science fiction. I once worked a summer job in an office where data was being punched onto cards by means of key punch machines. It has been a while since I've seen an IBM card.

When I began working for the Oregon Bureau of Labor and Industries, my main equipment was an electric typewriter. The agency did not yet have a word processing system, although I had seen such a system in large banks. It seemed to speed up the work remarkably. After a short while the state agency got the Wang word processing system. It could hold lots of data such as names, addresses, and numbers. One could write a letter, an article, or even a book on a word processor.

Of course, training was required, especially for those like me who had never touched a computer. Some employees were sent during working hours for their training. I got mine through evening classes at Portland Community College.

What had gone before the Wang system was now obsolete, much like the horse and buggy. Typos could be instantly corrected without a whiteout. The Carbon paper was unnecessary with a printer that could print as many copies as requested. This changed the face of office procedures. Then came the name of William Henry Gates III, born in Seattle in 1955. He is best known for the giant corporation called Microsoft and the computer system known as Windows. Wow! Windows brought pictures to the monitor screen. There were some sessions at work where everyone sat looking at a big screen in front while someone in the back projected pictures and charts on the screen. This system could do so many things, which the instructor ran through at what seemed like breakneck speed. It all seemed so confusing. I needed hands-on practice with this. We did have several hands-on sessions with each individual sitting with a monitor and a keyboard. After a while, we were using the Microsoft Windows system for our work. The Wang system was removed. It had been the Model T. We now had what was comparable to the modern automobile, and we were learning to drive it.

It took a little more time before the majority of households had a computer at home. I got my first home computer in August of 1998, and the program was Windows 98. For a while, I sat up past bedtime looking up information, reading articles, and using e-mail. The computer was a sleep stealer. I'm still dealing with the discipline of limiting how much time I spend on the computer versus other things that need to be done at home. Meanwhile, technology has advanced. Several computer programs have come and gone. I have had Windows 7 and Windows 10. Like my comparison with the automobile, most people drive, but they also know enough about cars that they understand when their cars must be taken for maintenance by professionals. Thus, we have computer programmers and computer technicians. We need to know when service is necessary, because crash is a heavy inconvenience.

A man by the name of Steven Paul Jobs, born in 1955 in San Francisco and died in 2014 in Palo Alto, California, built a corporation called Apple. His work led to further technology with tablets and smartphones. My son-in-law gave me a tablet. I practiced on it because it was smaller than my desktop computer and responded to a lighter touch than I was used to applying. Once I was trying to look up my bank account balance, but I messed up on the password several times, and my account was locked. I had to change my password, which I did the next morning with the help of the website chat.

It's hard to imagine my days before the computer. Information can be found so quickly. I can buy things online. I can keep up with events, I'm in touch with relatives and friends by e-mail, although for me, e-mail does not take the place of a phone call or a face-to-face chat.

Like any technological invention, the computer can be used for good or ill. It depends on what humans put into it. Garbage in means garbage out. Sadly, the computer has greatly increased the availability of porn. On the positive side, the computer has made it much easier to find help for problems, connect with people who share a common interest, and get a message out too many more people.

MUST I WAIT?

Time is so swift, and weeks roll on, it seems,
When things go well, as in fantastic dreams.
But where is the letter that has not come?
The job I asked for, which is yet to be done?
Oh, there is a day much more like a week
Or a week like a month, crawling so steep.
The silent seasons flow, holding not back.
Impatience comes unbidden to attack.
Who likes to have to wait when I must?
I'm told the day will come, and I must trust.
The prize is worth the wait, and when I see
Its treasured worth and comfort have given me,
I know the strength of patience day by day
To wait with courage, patience will repay.

A SUMMER DAY

Awakened by early sunrise
I look at the tasks I hope to do.
To finish these tasks is quite wise.
But the day must not pass from view
Without a kindness or a gentle word
To someone who waits for it to be heard.

AMY AND LAURA

Once upon a time, there were two little girls named Amy and Laura. They and their parents lived in a western coastal area. When Christmas came around, the song "White Christmas" was only a song about the New England winter scenes, which were the model for the Courier and Ives Christmas cards. Their father had grown up in Nebraska and sometimes sang a song about "Christmas Eve and the cold winds blow and the frozen ground is white with snow." It happened there, but not where they lived. Although they did not remember snow at Christmas, they knew that January usually brought a few days of snow when they could build a snowman. The adults did not like snow days because it was so hazardous to drive in a city unprepared for such weather.

One Christmas morning, Amy and Laura found a sled underneath the tree. "It won't be long until we can have some winter fun!" they exclaimed excitedly.

The days passed into January. There was rain, but no snow yet. One morning, Amy said to Laura, "I had a dream about a snowman. He asked if you and I could come to the mountains and visit him and play with our sled and also build him a playmate."

"I wish we could," replied Laura. "Do you suppose Mom and Dad would take us and our sled to the mountains on a weekend?"

At breakfast, Amy and Laura made their request.

"I'll tell you what," answered their father. "You girls do your homework and help your mother this week. I will check on my tire chains in the garage. They must be ready and in order. Then, Saturday will be a good day to go to your snowman on the mountain."

The following Saturday, when they arrived on the mountain, they found many people with sleds, toboggans, and skis. Amy and Laura rode down the slope on their sled. They joined with other children in building snow people, they made new friends. When they arrived home that evening, they thanked their parents for a day of fun.

CULTURE SHOCK

Created for beauty and bright glory,
God's marvelous and ever joyous story,
I live upon the earth, a world of woe,
Vandalized by sin and hate. Tears must flow.
Creator Whose mighty heart it broke,
You stepped into this misery and spoke
Of mercy and redemption, love and peace.
Perfect among sinners, you were slain,
But life arose to cleanse the crimson stain
Of one like me who yearns for your return.
E'en amid the chaos let your light burn.
Then you will reign as death and suffering cease.

WAR AND CONSEQUENCES

I was sixteen, in high school, and interested in what was happening in my nation and in the world.

Eleven years before this, the United States, Great Britain, and Russia had joined in a four-year war to take down the monstrous regime of Adolf Hitler in Germany. That regime had overrun most of Europe.

In February 1945, the American President Franklin Roosevelt, the British Prime Minister Winston Churchill, and the Russian Premier Josef Stalin met at Yalta to discuss the plans for Europe when the war ended. The end result was that Germany was divided into zones of oversight, American and British on the west and Russian on the east. Problems were soon readily apparent. Stalin had come to Yalta with firm plans for Russian rule over Poland. He also assumed control of Hungary, Romania, Czechoslovakia, and Bulgaria, and the Balkan states of Latvia, Lithuania, and Estonia.

The world view of humanity and human history held by Stalin and the Communist rulers was in stark contrast to the world view held by the West. It was based upon faith in a Creator and upon human rights and dignity. The United States set out to rebuild Europe after the war, and the Western European nations recovered and prospered. Communist Russia, on the other hand, had an economic system that kept most of the people poor. Thus, there began a long period of tension between the Soviet Union and the West. The western borders of the counties which Russia now controlled were sealed with barbed wire fences and towers with armed guards. Winston Churchill called this the Iron Curtain.

In the fall of 1956, some people in Hungary, motivated by the universal human craving for freedom, set up a government of their own. Within a few days, tanks from the east rolled in. The rebellion was quickly crushed. There were pictures in Life magazine of people kneeling over the bodies of loved ones in the streets. A few Hungarians managed to escape with little more than the clothes on their backs. In downtown Portland, Oregon, the Red Cross had a place where people could donate to help the Hungarian refugees. There was a tank in front of the place. It was the only time I have seen a real tank. The situation came closer when a refugee family – a couple with two children – moved into the house across the street from my family. - My church sponsored two refugee men and got them jobs.

Nine years later, I had the opportunity to travel to Europe with a group. We spent a month in Austria, each with an individual family. Then the group traveled in Austria and at one point came close to the Iron Curtain, looking past the barbed wire and onto the plain of Hungary. Then we went to Germany, to Berlin. In 1961, a 20-mile wall had been built between East and West Berlin. So many people had been escaping from Communist East Germany through West Berlin that the Communist rulers had to plug the hole. So, we saw the west side of the wall, with its memorial wreaths to people who had been shot in the attempt to escape over the wall.

I was twenty-five. I contemplated the wall and its symbolism. "Yes," I thought. Communism is powerful. But it denies God and denies an essential part of what makes us human. It will have to fall at some time, but that will be after my own lifetime on earth." Eventually came the autumn of 1989. I had not yet reached my

50th birthday. There had been news reports of a movement in Poland called Solidarity. Amazingly, stirrings erupted in other countries behind the Iron Curtain. One by one, these regimes fell. In November, people were dancing on top of the Berlin Wall. It was awesome!

Communism still exists in Asia. There is China with a billion people plus another United States of America. There is North Korea with a cruel regime with nuclear weapons. Vietnam, Laos, and Cambodia are still under Communist rule. Then there is Cuba. My prayer is, "Lord, you brought down Communism in Europe with a mighty hand. Will you do the same in Asia and in Cuba? Then, what will happen with radical Islam? You know, Lord. You know."

CHAINS

Chains bind one to a rock,
A rock of deep regret
that I can't satisfy
demands and other wants
In one large block.
Perhaps a day will bring

Some form of luck or joy,
Dispelling the shadows,
Showing the rock to be a dwarf,
Breaking the chains of sadness,
Causing the heart to sing.

THE EYE DOCTOR

In a public school in the late 1940s, it was rather common to see a child with a boil on the skin or a sty on the eyelid. Such infections, usually by Staphylococcus bacteria, are serious. However, antibiotics at the time were new. Penicillin was a marvel, labeled a "miracle drug" for the speed at which it cleared up infections. No one, not even the medical community, foresaw the emergence of what are now called "superbugs" with their resistance to the earlier antibiotics. So, a boil or a sty was routinely treated with penicillin, and hospital patients were routinely given penicillin as a preventive measure, whether or not there were symptoms of infection.

As an eight-year-old, I developed a sty on my left eyelid. My father took me to an eye specialist. The sty would have to be lanced and drained. That was a relatively simple procedure, but the doctor looked at me and at my father and said, "She probably will not sit still for what I have to do. She should probably go to the hospital."

The word "hospital" brought back memories of three years earlier when I had surgery on my neck. I was in the hospital for a few days, and twice each day, I got a shot in the spanking place. If I had been given any choice at all, I would have taken the spanking, of which I probably got fewer than I deserved.

"Please," I piped up. "I don't want to go to the hospital again. I'll sit still."

"I would have to give you one shot near your eyebrow to put your eye to sleep," the doctor explained. "Do you think you can sit still for that moment?"

"I'll do it. I promise," I replied.

So, I got into the chair, gripped the arms of the chair, and when the Novocain had been administered, I knew that the worst was over. That was the only shot I would get here. In the hospital, I was sure there would be more. I did not choose to have the sty, and with good, responsible parents, I had no choice about going for treatment. However, I could choose how to behave in the doctor's office. The doctor had given me that choice. I gripped the arms of the chair and did not scream or cry, and thus avoided the hospital. I surprised both the doctor and my father as the doctor applied ointment to my eyelid and a white gauze patch, which I wore according to instructions for three days. The sty healed.

As a child, I sometimes had ear infections. For this, our family doctor prescribed an elixir, which, to the best of my knowledge, was penicillin. It was brown in color, and the taste was agreeable enough that I called it chocolate medicine.

But there was another unforeseen problem with penicillin. When I was about 12, I broke out in a rash after being treated with the drug. Some people became allergic to it. By this time, there we other kinds of antibiotics.

Somewhere in every situation, human beings make choices. We have people who simply perceive themselves as victims to whom other people owe something. But we also have inspiring stories of people who seemed to have hit bottom, without hope, and then turned their lives around.

The words "victim" and" victor" each come from the same Latin verb "vincere", which means to conquer. Names such as Victoria, Victor, and Vincent mean "overcomer". But you can be an overcomer regardless of your name.

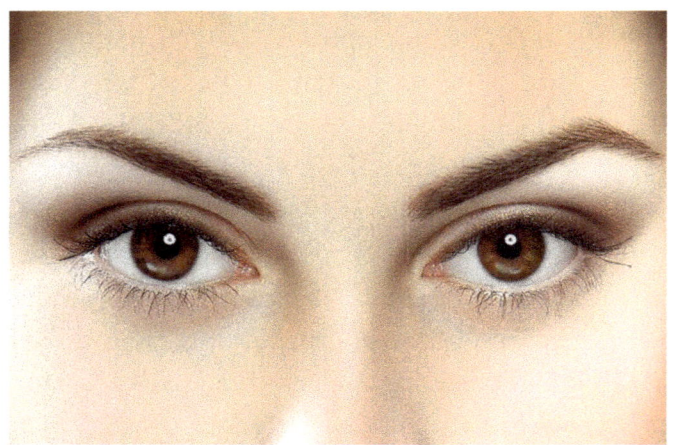

LIGHT

Sun, stars, galaxies
Rainbow spectrum of the light,
Eyes to gaze in awe.

See the shadows dark,
The sparkle of ocean waves,
The moon on the snow.

Marv'lous eye to see
The faces of loved ones joyous,
Gems, leaves and flowers.

NEW SETTING

A day's journey still in the world of man.
Will it be lonely? No! God is still here
As he has been since time began.
His children, I can meet and hold them dear.

I've come from challenges and yet been blessed
by family, beauty, wonders of the sky.
The sea and mountains, trees, and all the rest.
Friends and loved ones share joy and woe so nigh.

Was this new setting something I had planned?
No, it was decided through family needs,
And we could give each helping hand.
Circumstances change, and God plants seeds.

We strive and struggle; life brings joy and pain.
We work and laugh and learn, and naught is vain.

VOYAGE

A voyage to distant lands
Across an ocean vast
Takes me to awesome strands
When I arrive at last.
Upon the deck, the stars at night
Innumerable, their Creator's power
Display in wondrous light so white
For voyagers such as I who mark the hour.
Does that Creator yet see me
Upon this vast and shining sea?

HATE KILLS

Hate kills the soul of the hater.
Its poison twists the mind's reason
And doubles the pain felt later.
Hate mocks reason, for which the mind is made,
Erupts in violence, leaving so much pain
And tragedy for those who have no shade.
Oh, lift the voice of reason in our land.
Away with slander; let the truth prevail.
Truth makes us human. Let's join hands in hand.

TO A FRIEND

Wherever you may be this quiet night,
I sit remembering when our bond was formed.
My thoughts now wrap you in a velvet light
Emitted from a heart that once you warmed.

We walked together once; we talked; we thought.
We shared the joys of growing in God's grace.
For one short while, so much to me you brought.
We're now apart in time, apart in space.

In thoughts and prayers, I now remember you.
I hope I've warmed your life as you have mine.
Whatever life has cast our way of gold or blue,
May God's hand guide you and your life be renewed.

Perhaps one day you'll hear of me again.
May your heart lift, be you in joy or pain.

THE MOUNTAIN

The mountain stands majestic in the sun
On days when clear and cloudless air prevails.
More often, when heavy clouds their course do run
And rains the land for day to day assails

The peak is hidden from my mortal eyes.
Is it still thee? I'll never doubt its form
Still stands against the heavy skies
And waits for wind and cloud and sullen storm

To yield their gloom and fury to the morn
Of light and peace and permeating joy
When shade gives way to sight, renewed and reborn,
A beauty that no human can destroy.

When God at times seems hidden far away
He is still there to be my guide and stay.

THE AIRPORT

They sit or stand, doze or visit,
And finally stand at one single gate
In a few short hours to be set down
Half a world away.

What makes them
Brothers yet strangers
Fleeting sojourners on a speck of dust,
A speck and yet a world immense?

Some seek their kin.
Some realize their dreams. What dreams?
The dream of every man
To put his mark
Upon places yet unknown to himself.
For good or ill, to say to others,
"I am here. I also claim
A part of you and this place is dear to you
For my own, and leave you
A part of myself
And that land dearest to me
For your own,
A burden or blessing

To hurt or heal
To weaken or nourish
The dream of peace.

GOLDENWEDS

The years of love, of hope, and faith.
Of joy and struggle,
Friendship and laughter,
Now turn to gold.
May the God who said
Man should not be alone
Bless you and all your moments
With His everlasting love.

CHALK

Chalk yellow as pollen
Bringing sneezes so strong.
Hard like stone but wearing to dust.
Leaving a message of understanding
In a soft written word
Light as air.

KNOWLEDGE

We've seen a great light, so they say.
It began as a star through a strange new tube.
It showed images of bone
on plastic plates.
It brought us face to face with those
Removed by many miles.
It shows into our inner selves

Through gene and atom.
Miracle and monster,
Knowledge you are a torch
But in whose hands?

TWO WAYS

Hate
Bomb
Burn
Destroy
Love
Compassion
Outreach
Healing
Healing of what?
Healing of the self
And of our land.

ADVENTURE

The longer my journey. The more I will see.
The more that I see, the more I should learn.
When people I meet see grace in me,
May I grow in wisdom, and friendship earn.

When seeing the scenes made by God's own hand
And hearing the music of the birds and the brook
I stand in praise of this bountiful land,
and for ears to listen and eyes to look.
I will rejoice in the gift of life,

Capacity to love and laugh and sing
To overcome sorrow and woes and strife,
As each morn a good renewal can bring.

As I ponder these wonders to connect
Adventure brings what I did not expect.

SPEAK

To speak, to share what's on one's heart
Puts one at risk of scorn. From whom?
From one whose heart is marred by anger.
Put fear aside and speak to those
Who would learn from what you share?

The gift of speech belongs to humankind.
From a clean heart, the tongue forms gentle words.
Which comfort, uplift, and may admonish
To strengthen a soul's resolve to heighten
The impact of its hidden gifts.

NO MORE SMOKE

The world is choking
On the smoke from the fire
Of evil in unregenerate hearts.
Lord, put out the flame of sin
And give men hearts that do not smoke
But glow with light and warmth
From the current of the Holy Spirit.

I SEEK JOY

I seek joy
Not as an emotional high
But an inner delight in life.

I seek joy
A delight which only increases
The more it is shared.

I seek joy
A fountain that flows through me
To refresh those whose lives I touch,

I seek joy
Too rare in a world of pain.
A peace that conquers pain.

I seek joy
For it is that for which I was created
By Him Who is the source of joy.

FAITH

Faith seems just like
A jumbled jigsaw puzzle
With no discernible picture.
Then Christ takes hold
Who knows each piece
And fits them all together.

www.ingramcontent.com/pod-product-compliance
Lightning Source LLC
Chambersburg PA
CBHW051250120626
46547CB00014B/1875